Breath of Life

Celebrating the Gift of life

Finding God during a time of worldly crisis.

By

Natascha Williams

Published by Hemingway Publishers

Cover design By Deston Williams

ISBN: Printed in the United States

Dedication

—◆◈◆—

Without you, I would not be who I am today.

I would be lost without you.

To my Lord and Savior, Jesus Christ, who gave me the most precious gift of all: life and not just life but life more abundantly in you. I am overjoyed to be living this life with you at the center of everything.

To my loving and supportive husband, who has always been there for me through the highs and lows of life. You have been my best friend, mentor, teacher, and pastor. You have taught me so much, and I will be eternally grateful and loved. Thank you for everything.

To our two boys, who gave me purpose as a mother of amazing young men who want to do the right thing. I cannot imagine my life without you all. You have truly made my life more joyful and blessed. Thank God

To everyone who has gone through the same tragic moment as COVID-19 and is still wanting more out of life. We are in this together.

Heartfelt Message

Lord, I thank you for creating me and giving me your breath of life so that I can use my God-given gifts to spread your glory around the world. Just like Ezekiel prophesied to those dry bones, you raised a nation and a vast army to fulfill what you wanted to be done.

Thank you for being my Lord and Savior; I would not want it any other way. I am grateful that you protected me from the disease (COVID-19) and crisis that has gripped the entire world.

We must turn and accept that the world cannot be shielded solely by vaccination or a mask, but that we must place our hope and faith in you while we still have life and remain positive.

We need more than just restrictions lifted so that we can spend quality time together. We must seek a higher purpose for why we are here on this earth, as we were created for far more than the basic day-to-day activities we engage in every day. We must exist knowing what our true calling and purpose are in order to fulfill them.

I am blessed and thankful for the love and support I received while I was in my valley, in my lost and lack of confidence stages, and wondering if I am sure I wanted to pursue this path of life.

My loving husband, for his love and support in allowing God to use him to reveal who I was in Christ and for encouraging me to pursue the greatness God had placed within me.

To my eldest son, who elevated my vision for my book cover to new heights of creativity. You are a gifted young man who has been a source of inspiration for me.

To my youngest son, who cheered me on all the way. Believing in me and doing whatever it took to allow me to focus on my work.

Sure! I am glad I did because God is allowing me and using me right now to set his people free.

If you are reading this, you are still in the race of life. We still have work to finish.

Praise the Lord for all of his great works, both past and future.

Thank goodness, his time of refreshment has arrived.

Table of Contents

Page Blank Intentionally

Introduction

❮◆❯

Ezekiel 37

"The hand of the Lord was upon me, and he brought me out in the Spirit of the LORD and set me down in the middle of the valley; it was full of bones. And he led me around among them, and behold, there were very many on the surface of the valley, and behold, they were very dry. And He said to me, "Son of man, can these bones live?"

And I answered, "O Lord GOD, you know."

Then he said to me, "Prophesy over these bones, and say to them, O dry bones, hear the word of the LORD. Thus says the Lord God to these bones: Behold, I will cause breath to enter you, and you shall live. And I will lay sinews upon you, and will cause flesh to come upon you, and cover you with skin, and put breath in you, and you shall live, and you shall know that I am the Lord."

So I prophesied as I was commanded. And as I prophesied, there was a sound, and behold a rattling, and the bones came together, bone to its bone. And I looked, and behold, there were sinews on them, and flesh come upon them, and skin had covered them. But there was no breath in them. Then he said to me, "Prophesy to the breath; prophesy, son of man, and say to the breath, Thus says the Lord God: Come from the four winds, O breath, and breathe on

1

these slain, that they may live." So I prophesied as he commanded me, and the breath came into them, and they lived and stood on their feet, an exceedingly great army.

Then he said to me, "Son of man, these bones are the whole house of Israel. Behold, they say, 'Our bones are dried up, and our hope is lost; we are indeed cut off.' Therefore prophesy, and say to them, Thus says the Lord God: Behold, I will open your graves and raise you from your graves, O my people. And I will bring you into the land of Israel. And you shall know that I am the LORD, when I open your graves, and raise you from your graves, O my people. And I will put my Spirit within you, and you shall live, and I will place you in your own land. Then you shall know that I am the LORD; I have spoken, and I will do it, declares the Lord."

Just like Ezekiel witnessed those dry bones, we were lifeless, without the breath that gave us life and the purpose to be human. God took each and every lifeless bone, formed and shaped our very being, and gave us the breath of Life. That is why we are all here today. We have to be so thankful for his marvelous works and for allowing us to be alive.

How God Created Mankind

Breathe in and breathe out the air we cannot see or feel, but we know we are receiving it as it sends oxygen throughout our bodies, letting us know we are alive. Without this breath, we would not have our existence. However, we know that we live and have our being through God: "For in him we live and move and have our being;" **(Acts 17:28)**. Realizing the importance of this breath we take will change our total outlook on life itself.

"For you formed my inward parts; you knitted me together in my mother's womb. I praise you, for I am fearfully and wonderfully made. Wonderful are your works; my soul knows it very well. My frame was not hidden from you when I was being made in secret, intricately woven in the depths of the earth. Your eyes saw my unformed substance; in your book were written every one of them, the days that were formed for me, when as yet there was none of them." **(Psalms 139:13-16)**

There are so many deep searches for questions that many may want to know about. I always wanted to know who Jesus was and why he was important to my life. There are many questions, like if God is more significant than I am, what does he need from poor little me? When you begin to ask the questions, you look, you listen, and you feel, the answers will surely come. I started off looking at creation. I read about the creation of Mankind and how God is our Father and gave us this gift we have today called "Life," and the picture became more evident to me. The importance of God as my Creator and life-giver. Once I sought out how sin came into the world and what sin was, I began to see how I needed Christ to save my soul because I was guilty and needed to partake of his salvation.

He provided to those who would believe, repent, and be changed. The world was made, and seeing it relates as we read how God created the world in just a few days. We see things beginning to make sense, and we get a better understanding of everything.

So, when I began to think of life itself and how God expresses how he created us "Fearfully and wonderfully." I would say he thought this out and was careful and wise in putting us together. Just look at how the human body was formed: the nerves, bones, and how everything was intricately woven together. Each body part has its function, helping another. Who can overlook the mesmerizing beauty of how God created our minds? I am amazed every time I think about the autonomy of the human body.

I love to walk in nature. When we read the beginning of Genesis, we see how God created the world. I think he is so wise, how he created everything and put it all in place: the sun, the moon, stars, and animals in the sea and on land. Then, he made his most precious masterpiece, humanity.

God formed each one of us by his hands out of the dust of the ground. "Then the LORD God formed the man of dust from the ground and breathed into his nostrils the breath of life, and the man became a living creature." (**Genesis 2:7**).

The question being asked here is, were we created out of the dust? But then, how do we come out of our mother's womb and not directly out of the ground? I totally understand the need for clarity here, as it makes sense because when we come out of the womb, we aren't dusty. However, God knew us before we were knitted in our mother's womb.

Jeremiah 1:5 states, "Before I formed you in the womb I knew you, and before you were born, I consecrated you; I appointed you a prophet to the nations."

So, this demonstrates the process before we came into our mother's womb. God knew us before. What we were like before is left to our imagination, but we know what happened after we came to the world as babies. We have the evidence of the breath of life in us. We are the evidence of his handiwork.

The word of God is here to edify and to be a witness to this fact. "All Scripture is breathed out by God and profitable for teaching, for reproof, for correction, and for training in righteousness."(**2 Timothy 3:16**).

We have to have faith to make it through each day and to decide what we believe in. God, being who he is, appreciates the precious gift he gave to us. We should also love the giver, who sets everything in motion.

If it weren't for God, there would be no plan B; he is the initial plan from the beginning to the end.

We must be grateful for our breath because it simply means we are alive; we are here, and God has a purpose for each one of us to manifest.

When we saw the lifelessness of the dry bones, we too were lifeless, but once Ezekiel was told to Prophesy to the four-wind, it entered into them, and life was fulfilled. **(Ezekiel 37:9-10).**

We must be so grateful that God is the giver of life and the one who can take it away.

"If he should set his heart to it and gather to himself his spirit and his breath, all flesh would perish together, and man would return to dust" **(Job 34: 14-15).**

This is a powerful message right here that God has all control over life and death. It is imperative to know as we begin to increase our knowledge as this is the beginning of fearing the Lord: "The fear of the Lord is the beginning of knowledge; fools despise wisdom and instruction."**(Prov 1:7)**. The beginning of wisdom is that we gain knowledge first and then apply understanding so that we gain the wisdom to apply the things we learned to our lives.

We gain the fear of God, which is to be careful and circumspect in what we say and do. When we love and respect someone, we trust that they are looking out for our best interest, so we follow suit and do what they ask of us. We become wiser in how we are to live our lives for him.

Because if we fear God we want to do what is right by him. We wouldn't want to hurt or go against him because we love him. So we walk with that in mind watching everything we do, and speak. Getting to know him more and more so, we are wiser.

He has the power to take it all back. The fact that you are here is a miracle; to be human is an honor because God gave us a part of him, so we have the most favorable gift we ever could receive. We are to celebrate and be grateful for this.

Let's connect: It is so great to know that we were created to be unique, gifted, and with purpose. I love to know that a loving God took his time with us, giving us the air we breathe, and now we are a living being because of him. I am so happy and excited to be alive.

Let's talk about it:

What were your thoughts about how you were created before reading this book?

How has this newfound truth changed your perspective on life?

Does this make you want to have a closer relationship with God?

What are some things you can do now to gain a better relationship with God?

The Gift of Life

---◆→●←◆---

"The Spirit of God has made me, and the breath of the Almighty gives me life." **(Job 33:4)**.

Say it with me: "I am Alive." Scream that with all of your being because it's truly a blessing to still be here after all we went through.

God, so majestic and supreme, imparted a big part of himself when he gave us the breath we now use to stay alive.

Similar to Ezekiel, who witnessed the lifeless bones come back to life. We recall our brother in Christ Job who went through so many trials and tribulations which came to test his faith. Just like what we've been through, his world was turned upside down, too. But we see through great strength in his faith that Job overcame loss and sickness and won the victory. He went through so much that he even questioned his own existence, but he stayed firm in his faith in God.

We, too can testify to the fact we faced a big attack that came and changed the entire world. We've seen people in the grief of losing their loved ones to COVID-19 and witnessing people getting sick. The changes made such as isolation, wearing masks, and social distancing. We went through our own trials and tribulations, but through everything, just like Job we have overcome by the grace of God.

We are living testimonies that we were handmade by God, and life exists because he gave us our existence and purpose for being here today. We, humans, were created far more than just to survive and to meet our daily needs but for a far greater purpose that God has us here for.

Life shouldn't be taken for granted, but with every inhale and exhale, we must be grateful we are still here to witness life and gain knowledge and understanding of what God has done, who he is, and what he truly means to us.

We witnessed the effect COVID-19 had on the entire world and that it came to attack the very thing God gave us: the breath of life. During this tragic time, we were all so frantic to make sure we didn't catch this infectious disease. It was a scary time for many when I witnessed the eagerness to rush out of shopping places to avoid touching anything so that we wouldn't get infected or make sure to maintain social distancing. All this was done while wearing masks, which were hard to breathe in.

The eagerness to stay alive was very active. Life was definitely on our minds. It definitely was on mine. However, now that we've gone through it, let us be mindful that if we are removed from existence, we can no longer be used here on earth for God's purpose.

"Many are the plans in the mind of a man, but it is the purpose of the Lord that will stand." **(Proverbs 19:21)**.

God is the giver and taker of life – "And the dust returns to the earth as it was, and the spirit returns to God who gave it" **(Ecclesiastes 12:7)**. His purpose for mankind is to live in fellowship with him, partaking in his creation and providing to us the care of the earth as he gave to us to have dominion over it.

In **Genesis 1:26-** "Then God said, "Let us make man in our image, after our likeness. And let them have dominion over the fish of the sea and over the birds of the heavens and over the livestock and over all the earth and over every creeping thing that creeps on the earth."

God depends on mankind to govern over earthly affairs, as it states

"Thus says the LORD: Heaven is my throne, and earth is my footstool;" **(Isaiah 66:1)**

As God has ordained each one of us, he created each one to have dominion; dominion means "Sovereignty over something." We were created for his purpose: that together, we'd join our will to fulfill God's heavenly will on earth.

That is why we say, "Thy kingdom come, your will be done, on earth as it is in heaven." _ **(Matthew 6:10)**. God depends on human relationships to establish his kingdom here on Earth, which is why we truly only have access to earthly affairs and not the heavenly realm.

We should be mindful of the fact that life is a gift as we watch the very first thing a baby does: take his first actual breath as he comes into the world from his mother's womb.

1 Peter 2:9 - It states, "But you are a chosen race, a royal priesthood, a holy nation, a people for his own possession, that you may proclaim the excellencies of him who called you out of darkness into his marvelous light."

There is so much purpose and greatness that God has invested in us. Once we acknowledge that life is a gift, we must also know that we were created for a purpose greater than ourselves. Greatness is in us all who choose to have this relationship with him and work in partnership with God.

As we begin to know our heavenly father, we begin to find out who we are in him. Who would have thought I would have so many ideas for books within me or that I have written so many beautiful songs inside of me? I can speak to nations and use my gifts to give God glory and fulfill his will on earth. We have so much inside of us we must give to others.

We believe this because he quickened us with life. And your life can be purposeful and pleasing to him if you connect deeply with our heavenly father. And knowing that we are his creation, we will praise him with all of our body, soul and mind. After all, he is the reason we are alive.

Let's connect: I love a good gift, something thoughtful and helpful for my life. The gift of life is by far the greatest gift I have ever received. God created me in his image for his kingdom. I pray to live each day faithfully for his glory.

Let's talk about it:

Have you ever pondered on the effects COVID-19 had on your life?

Have you considered why you are still alive differently since experiencing COVID-19?

Have you wondered or looked into what your purpose in God is? If so, what is stopping you from fulfilling your calling in God?

What would you like to do differently to live your life intentionally?

Taking care of our body as it is his temple

"What? Know ye not that your body is the temple of the Holy Ghost which is in you, which ye have of God, and ye are not your own? For ye are bought with a price: therefore glorify God in your body, and in your spirit, which are God's." **(1 Corinthians 6: 19-20 KVJ)**

God thought of everything; he created the earth, breathed life into mankind, and even provided us with the means to eat. I can just imagine his initial plan and purpose, as he stated in **Genesis 1: 29**— And God said, "Behold, I have given you every plant yielding seed that is on the face of all the earth and every tree with seed in its fruit. You shall have them for food."

God is a God of abundance to provide us with the necessities of food, but to give us its seed simply means we'd continue to have it abundantly. As we know, if we plant the seed of an Apple tree, it will bear plenty of fruit.

We must appreciate God's initial plan for our eating habits and choices. Taking care of our bodies will sustain us and give us longevity. Plus, if you do this, it will provide you with energy, strength, and joy to keep on keeping on.

We have access to all the plants yielding seed and every tree with seed in its fruit. He also advised us in Genesis 9:3, "Every moving thing that lives shall be food for you. And as I gave you the green plants, I give you everything."

He shall provide our needs, and he has done it. However, everything is available to us; things should be done in moderation because too much of something isn't always a wise choice. Take care of your body as in **1 Corinthians 6: 19-20** "Or do you not know that your body is a temple of the Holy Spirit within you, whom you have from God? You are not your own, for you were bought with a price. So, glorify God in your body."

Once we begin our journey in the Lord and accept him in our hearts and lives, he won't leave us walking this journey alone. He will send you his Holy Spirit, which is to guide and comfort you in good and hard times, to communicate through you to speak to God.

When we consider our body to be a temple, it is a sacred place for the spirit to dwell in. Therefore, we think about how we treat ourselves and take good care of ourselves because we have more to live for, as God surely wants us to be mindful of these things.

There are so many things God is interested in, and what we choose to put into our body is one. God can use you when you have life, and we know that there are clearly things we can indulge in that can cause harm. "For none of us liveth to himself, and no man dieth to himself." **(Romans 14:7)**

I am clearly not a dietitian, but I am mindful of keeping myself healthy by trying to make good, healthy choices. "For anyone who eats and drinks without discerning the body eats and drinks judgment on himself." **(1 Corinthians 11:29)**. We have to be mindful of everything we put inside ourselves. God cares, and so should we. I can drink alcohol, but I care too much about the parts of my body that can get affected and damaged. There are so many things I can choose to indulge myself in but my choices have to be wise as it can cost me sickness or my life. Which one is more important to us?

Being intentional about what we choose to put in our bodies can help us remain energized, as we are given food that supplies that great source of energy. Then there are foods that cause us harm, make us sluggish, and put on excessive weight. Let us not forget about what we drink, as it can also damage our internal organs, which sometimes doesn't always alarm us when in distress.

Meaning that sometimes that drink could be our last because of severe damage to the liver.

Our minds, bodies, and spirits all need to be nourished well. Once we know who we are, we can walk with purpose and dignity. I truly believe that knowledge is power, and God states it best: "My people are destroyed for lack of knowledge." **(Hosea 4:6)**. It is good to find out what is best for us and take steps to be mindful of what we choose to put in our bodies.

We know that if we have a luxurious car, we won't put just any regular gasoline in it, but the right gasoline that will make your car work best and give it longevity. This is the same concept for mankind, even though we have so many choices to put inside of us. Everything isn't good for us, we should take care of ourselves to live out our best years of being healthy, strong, and happy.

Let's connect: There is so much we can do, but not everything is the right thing to do. I love my body, mind, and soul too much to allow anything to go into it. I want the place where the Spirit of God resides to be clean, healthy and active so I can be used purposefully and for a long time.

Let's talk about it:

What are your thoughts on your body being the temple for God?

Having this knowledge now, how has this changed your lifestyle?

What hesitations do you have about making changes to your lifestyle?

What are some ways you can involve God to help you in your daily choices?

Taking care of our mental health

—◆◆●◆◆—

"Do not be anxious about anything, but in everything by prayer and Supplication with thanksgiving let your requests be made known to God. And the peace of God, which surpasses all understanding, will guard your hearts & your minds in Christ Jesus. **(Phillippians 4:6-7)**

From the beginning of time when mankind fell, you can see the effect this has caused mentally, spiritually, emotionally, and physically.

God provided mankind (Adam & Eve) with the truth, and they neglected this fact for a lie; choosing their own will and desires, they went against God and disobeyed him.

What hurts us the most when it comes to our mindset is the things we choose to believe and do. Much of the pain is caused by thoughts of mistakes or events that keep replaying in our minds, causing us too many painful memories and, therefore affecting how we live our lives.

Imagine the effect this had on our first ancestors, who turned against their creator, carrying a heavy weight of sin to come into the world. They were ashamed because they hid and were afraid. They were given the rightful consequences for their actions but had to live a much harder life. So, their actions had a significant effect on them.

We transform ourselves by renewing our minds, holding onto those things that are factual and true. I've gone through a lot of painful things in my life, and when I think about them, it causes me to be either sad or upset.

When I looked deeper into why I felt this way, I saw that many things I went through left me feeling abandoned by those who left or let down by myself or others. However, to change how I view things now is to know that what I went through did happen, so I accepted this and realized that I needed to be more graceful in myself. If I knew better, I would do better.

So, I renewed the way I viewed my past but acknowledged what I went through, learning from it so I can give myself wisdom today and know that today I am not alone as God was always with me, and though the Devil wanted to sift me like wheat he wasn't able to as I am still here. So, I am grateful to God for bringing me from where I came from to be where I am today. It is because of his grace and his mercy that I can stand. After all, he says, "We are more than conquerors" (**Romans 8:37**). Walk in that integrity and truth, my dear friends.

We hear every day that Mental health is so important, and I agree with this saying because what we think about affects the way we conduct ourselves.

That is why the scripture says in **Proverbs 23:7 KJV**. " For as he thinketh in his heart, so he is," We process the thoughts from our minds and then act them out through our hearts. This is why we have to know God by reading his word, and praying to him to get a better understanding of "Finally, brethren, whatsoever things are true, whatsoever things are honest, whatsoever things are just, whatsoever things are pure, whatsoever things are lovely, whatsoever things are of good report; if there be any virtue, and if there be any praise, think on these things." **(Philippians 4:8)**.

That's it. We've been through a lot, but now we can pause and take a deep breath, reflecting on the good things we are thankful for, such as life, health, safety, shelter, and so much more.

God needs our mind because out of it, he communicates, gives us visions, and ideas for creativity and helps guide us. "I appeal to you, therefore, brothers, by the mercies of God, to present your bodies as a living sacrifice, holy and acceptable to God, which is your spiritual worship. Do not be conformed to this world, but be transformed by the renewal of your mind, that by testing you may discern what is the will of God, what is good and acceptable and perfect. **(Romans 12:1-2)**

What we think about can affect how we act because we can go and do the things we are visualizing in our minds, and it can affect how we feel. Because we can think of a lot of hurtful things that keep us down or upset, and not feeling encouraged at all. Therefore, we become unhealthy and live in our sinful, fleshy ways. "Set your mind on things that are above, not on things that are on Earth." **(Colossians 3:2)**.

Such as the things we seek after that will rot and wither away. The things we deem important and invest so much value but aren't as valued in the kingdom of God.

The things of God are eternal, have a greater expectancy, and are more rewarding. When we seek to gain earthly possessions and spend so much strength and thought on getting these things, we aren't depositing enough investments in the things of God he mentions here: "Do not lay up for yourselves treasures on earth, where moth and rust destroy and where thieves break in and steal, but lay up for yourselves treasures in heaven, where neither moth nor rust destroys and where thieves do not break in and steal. For where your treasure is, there your heart will be also." **(Matthew 6:19-21)**.

If we align our thoughts with God's ways, we can walk holy and righteous before him. We can do his will because we know what he wants us to do. Every part of ourselves, including the state of our mental, emotional, spiritual, and physical being, is important to God.

All of our being is important because God needs all of us so he can use us. Mentally, he can communicate visions and ideas and provide us with creativity. Emotionally, we need to be sober-minded, as God's fruit of the Spirit, to mention a few, is Joy, peace, and above all, Love.

"Since we have these promises, beloved, let us cleanse ourselves from every defilement of body and spirit, bringing Holiness to completion in the fear of God." **(2 Corinthians 7:1)**

Physically so that we are fully capable of running the race of life and enduring until the end. "Do you not know that in a race, all the runners run, but only one receives the prize? So run that you may obtain it. Every athlete exercises self-control in all things. They do it to receive a perishable wreath, but we an imperishable. So I do not run aimlessly; I do not box as one beating the air. But I discipline my body and keep it under control, last after preaching to others I myself should be disqualified." **(1 Corinthians 9:24- 27)**.

We have to take excellent care of our entire being. For example, look at the Apostle Paul in the Bible before he met Christ. He was murdering the Christians following and preaching Christ. He didn't believe in God as he didn't have a mindset that would live and honor God to respect others serving the Lord and sparing their lives.

He didn't have the mindset of knowing the true and living God personally; therefore, emotionally, he didn't love God, nor was he a believer, as he was fetching them to kill them. He thought he was doing service to God. Physically, he was an oppressor, and he defiled himself.

The scripture says, "And he said, What comes out of a person is what defiles him. For from within, out of the heart of man, come evil thoughts, sexual immorality, theft, murder, adultery, coveting, wickedness, deceit, sensuality, envy, slander, pride, foolishness. All these evil things come from within, and they defile a person."

(Mark 7:20-23)

He changed when he witnessed Christ and met him alone, allowing him to know the truth. From the encounter, he changed from a murderer to a mighty, anointed man of God preaching the same gospel he was against. He dedicated his life to servitude and preaching God's word, saving many lives.

He had to transform his mind from a lie to the truth. Let's go over this together so it is true that Paul was a murderer that he was guilty of. He received the revelation of Christ which, therefore, had a transformation on how he thought. He was converted to a righteous man with the aid of the Spirit of God to equip him. He was taught what was right and that made him walk right, not to fulfill his will on earth, killing anymore, but by giving people life by giving them the salvation of Christ. He then had a mindset that now set out to fulfill the will of God and spread the gospel for God's kingdom.

With this change of mindset, we see that him being filled with the Spirit of God. He was now able to allow his thoughts in his mind to be of God, and his actions followed by his wanting to fulfill the will of God and his desires aligned with God's word now.

The transformation is real, and sometimes others wouldn't believe you are even the same person how you went from night to day, but it can happen to all of us. God is loving and merciful to help us in all of our times of need. Every area of our being he is interested in, so don't ever think that your issues are too much for him because it isn't.

We need to heal once we gain this knowledge because knowledge is power, right? However, even though knowledge is power indeed, to be effective, we must apply this great knowledge to see its full effectiveness. The more we learn and understand, the more we see right and wrong, and we'll be amazed. "For in much wisdom is much grief: and he that increaseth knowledge increaseth sorrow **(Ecclesiastes 1:18 KJV)**

Our purpose and first commandment is that we are to love the Lord your God with all your heart, and with all your soul and with all your mind. This is the excellent and first Commandment. "Master, which is the great commandment in the law? Jesus said unto him, Thou shalt love the Lord thy God with all your heart, and with all thy soul, and with all thy mind. This is the first and greatest commandment. And the second is like unto it, thou shalt love thy neighbor as thyself." (Matthew **22: 36-38 KJV**) The mind is an essential part of our being and is necessary to God because we have to use it to glorify him. "What am I to do? I will pray with my spirit, but I will pray with my mind also; I will sing praise with my spirit, but I will sing with my mind also." (**1 Corinthians 14:15**).

We should praise Him with every part of our physical body.

God wants every part of our being to use us for his glory, being part of his great inheritance, so that we all will be called the children of God. "See what kind of love the Father has given us, that we should be called children of God; and so we are. The reason why the world does not know us is that it did not know him." (**1 John 3:1**).

So, take good care of your mental health, replacing it with God's faith, his everlasting love for you, and his truth, which is his divine purpose for who you are, why you are here on earth, and how you came to existence.

Take great walks outside and admire nature, connecting with the sun and earth God provided. Read inspirational and motivational books that will give you better insight and strength to keep on going. Especially the bible, which can give you a better understanding and revelation on all things of God. Dance and live, get up and move your body, letting it praise the Lord for all he has done for you. Rest and get good sleep. He hopes for your future and strengthens you to fight the good fight. Provides goodness to be righteous, peace to live holy in his abounding grace.

A lot of times, we are wounded and broken, but God doesn't despise a crushed spirit. "The sacrifices of God are a broken spirit; a broken and contrite heart, O God, you will not despise." **(Psalm 51:17)**. You have to surrender the hurt and pain to the only one who understands because he says, "Casting all your anxieties on him because he cares for you." **(1 Peter 5:7)**. We need to render our heart to God. He cares and loves us with everlasting love, just that we must believe to receive his love.

Let's connect: We should speak so kindly about our mental health. There is so much that people go through, and God knows this. He cares for our state of mind and helps us through this life to have better mental health.

I remember a time in my life when I was either stuck in my past mentally or going to the future to peek at what was to come. However, I learned not to worry but to live each day as it comes. The pains of the past happened, but don't allow them to keep on hurting your present moment. It is far too precious. Remember that.

Let's talk about it:

Were you someone who struggled with events that happened in your life?

How important is taking care of your mental health after reading this section?

What steps are you willing to take to address your struggles?

Knowing that our mental health matters to God, what changes can help you get closer to God?

Establishing a relationship with God

— ◆◉◆ —

"Fight the good fight of the faith. Lay hold on eternal life, whereunto thou art also called, and hast professed a good profession before many witnesses. I give thee charge in the sight of God, who quickeneth all things, and before Christ Jesus, who before Pontius Pilate witnessed a good confession; that thou keep this commandment without spot, unrebukeable, until the appearing of our Lord Jesus Christ: which in his times he shall shew, who is the blessed and only Potentate, the King of Kings, and the Lord of lords; who only hath immortality, dwelling in the light which no man can approach unto; whom no man hath seen, nor can see: to whom be honour and power everlasting... Amen **(1 Timothy 6:12-16)**

In the dictionary, the word "relationship" means to have a connection or association, The condition of being related.

At this point, we acknowledge that we have an association with God as our heavenly Father, who is the one who created and formed us, providing the breath that we breathe. We all fell from his grace, even though we aren't Adam and Eve, we have to say that the effect of their actions has caused all of humanity to be shamed by the effect of sin.

According to **Romans 3:23**, which says, "For all have sinned and fall short of the glory of God." We are all mentioned in this scripture, so based on this, we had to be reconciled back to a relationship with God. What came between us was that we are now stained and unholy due to our sins. However, with God constantly having us on his mind, he had a plan that could save humanity and establish a relationship once again.

"For God so loved the world, that he gave his only Son, that whoever believes in him should not perish but have eternal life." **(John 3:16)**

He sent his only begotten son to be spared on a cross to cleanse us with his pure blood, for Christ was a man without any sin. He came in the flesh, but he was holy and is the way to the Father. Do you believe what is being told to you? It should make a lot of sense at this point.

Why does God need a relationship? God has desires, and one of them is "The Lord is not slow to fulfill his promise as some count slowness, but is patient toward you, not wishing that any should perish, but that all should reach repentance." **(2 Peter 3:9)**.

For us to be in good standing with God, we first have to own up to our offenses and plead guilty before him so that Jesus, who already died for our sins, can advocate for us and forgive us of our sins. Still, if you don't know them or even own up to being convicted of an offense, you can go on in life just continuing in them and offending your heavenly father and not fully receiving the salvation Jesus offers to each man.

We can have a relationship because we know first who he is: God our Father. Who we are is his creation, his handiwork, which he formed from the earth himself. Providing us with this spirit, we are to be connected with him in how we live our lives, seeking to please him, fearing him because we respect him, and loving him because we want to fulfill his will in our lives.

We need to love him, honor our parents, and love ourselves as we would our neighbors. Living in a brotherly and sisterly way.

From the beginning, God established a relationship with us. Imagine when Adam had dominion and was in charge and was given authority over the animals and earthly affairs.

Disobedience came in between our relationship with him. For we followed the things of the world, wanting more than what God gave us. The snake advised Eve that she would be like God, knowing right from wrong, but that is why we mustn't fall into an identity crisis and accept a lie for the truth.

God created us in his image and likeness. There is no identity crisis when you know, you know. Get knowledge, then understand and apply the wisdom.

Once you know this knowledge, you are to act upon it and become the children of God he initially had planned from the beginning of time. Then, we won't be facing or walking this life alone because God will be with us every step of the way.

Let's connect: I think having a relationship with God is extremely important. We can find everything we need in him. He is the wisest, kindest, and most loving God, and we can benefit most from his relationship. Isn't it good to belong, to be considered? God had such a great plan for us that he wanted all of us to be included. What greater time to connect with him, knowing he is our safe place and we can get all we need from him.

Let's talk about it:

How do you feel about your relationship with God today?

How do you show up daily to demonstrate you are a child of God?

Is there any area of your walk in God you'd like to strengthen, and how?

If you don't have a relationship with God, what do you think is hindering you?

The air we breathe being Contaminated by Covid 19 (My Testimony)

Just to think that we did all we could to avoid getting COVID - 19. We followed all the protocols, disinfected ourselves, wore masks, and even took all the vaccinations available. That still didn't prevent us from catching this infectious disease.

We didn't end up getting COVID-19 from outside; it crept into our home. Our youngest son came home with what was considered a cold, but later that night, it turned into a hot fever, and he then had an awful cough.

COVID-19 came to kill, steal, and destroy, but the blood of Jesus stands against it. Our son was tested, and he caught the virus. It affected all of us differently. Let me explain....

When I got COVID-19, it felt like it attacked my nervous system. My body was weak immediately; I felt so fatigued and slept so much, and my body and muscles felt so weak. When I would walk, it was so hard, and it was as if I had to learn to walk all over again.

When I got the cough, my chest would hurt; it was awful and painful. My body was so weak, and my immune system was under attack. It was a trying time for everyone in our household.

It also removed one of my senses, which was the sense of smell. I could smell something I thought was COVID-19, but it was tough to smell naturally.

When I lost one of my senses, it made me realize how much I needed them all. For they are all useful and when it was hard to smell the roses, it was tough because I love to stop and smell the roses.

It was a trying time for us, and my body was under attack; I went from sleeping so much to not sleeping at all. I was praising the Lord one night, and as I lay there, my chest hurt from the coughing. I felt the Holy Spirit's fire melt COVID away, and the worship song began playing as I listened to music. It was about the fire of the Holy Ghost.

He is nearer to us than we think. When we were walking through the valley of the shadow of death, I was overwhelmed with the fear of this illness taking my life. I only had faith, and God saw me through. My household and I are conquerors of COVID-19 by the grace of God.

God healed me and my family, and he proved that once we depend and count on him, he will never let us down. He will be there for us, and if you keep on holding on to his hand, you will see him in the darkest parts of your life. You didn't think he was there, so stay true to his promise.

Personally, this is my testimony while having COVID-19; however, I know that there are so many stories that ended tragically, and countless lives were taken due to this disease.

I had thoughts of death, thinking, would I or the kids and my husband make it, and we all did, by the mercy and blood of Jesus.

Gladly, we are still here to share our story with you all.

Trust in God and believe he is your final say and healer. Also, listen to your body. If it needs rest, food, spirituality, laughter, and love, give it what it needs.

We couldn't have made it if it wasn't for Jesus being with us, Healing and delivering us, and God the Father showing us so much love, mercy and grace. The Holy Spirit's comforting us and doing the work within us to kick COVID out of us; praise the Lord. Our faith and hope to live and not die: "I shall not die, but live, And declare the works of the LORD" **(Psalm 118:17).** Our loving tribe, our family unit at home, looking out for each other as COVID-19 affected us all differently. We had support for each other all the way. Thanks to online shopping places who brought us all the items we needed when we couldn't go outside.

We love and comfort all those who didn't make it or are going through it. Put God first and watch him take over your life for the betterment of things to come.

As I write this book, after all the years that passed since the pandemic, we still have to guard ourselves because just this year, sometime, someone from my household caught the virus again. So, we need to still stay vigilant and keep ourselves safe.

My family members are better than ever, but it was hard to go through this again; once again, I just laid my hands on him and prayed for his healing, saying, "You are going to be alright." Activating my faith that I trusted God to be our healer, and great physician in this time of need. Thank God for his peace, which keeps us resting on his everlasting arms.

Let's connect: Dear Friends, we all have a story worth sharing. We'd be amazed at how inspiring and uplifting our story can be to others who need it.

Let's talk about it:

Have you ever reflected on your experience during COVID-19?

What is your testimony? Can you share what God did for you?

How did you witness God helping during this time?

How would you say your relationship has grown in God?

Peace during times of sickness

"Now may the Lord of peace himself give you peace at all times in every way. The Lord be with you all" *(2 Thessalonians 3:16)*

What is peace during a time of the unknown, pain, and fear? The dictionary defines it as a state of tranquility and harmony.

During a time when our life is threatened with sickness, so many thoughts come to our minds. What if this and that happens, and the news doesn't help as it continues mentioning another person passing due to COVID-19?

Your time seems to run fast as you think about the state of your life. I think once you know your life is in the hands of the Lord, all your worries go to him. We trust the Lord to make the best life decisions so we don't have to worry about it. He knows everything and is the wisest one to seek from because, after all, he is the answer.

We should trust him, "Casting all your anxieties on him, because he cares for you." **(1 Peter 5:7).** The God who created our very being can give us the things we need, and he knows the fate of our life." We have to trust him with our fears, anxieties, and worries.

As long as we give him our life, we won't be afraid to lose it because it is in him. The word says, "for" In him we live and move and have our being." **(Acts 17:28)**

That is why when my whole household fell sick with COVID-19, I was feeling fragile. We all felt the fear that we wouldn't make it with this deadly disease, which had taken so many lives already. God showed up for all of us, and during this time of fear and sadness, he turned sadness into a song and fear into a dance.

He delivered and healed us in the mighty name of Jesus Christ. We overcame, and he was with us throughout the whole time, constantly proving himself to be there for us.

Peace is vital in our lives because it gives us the opportunity to go on cruise control and let Jesus be the driver, taking care of things. We are so used to being worried, having control, and figuring it all out.

I know just thinking back through all we've been through in the last years. It can be so overwhelming, but breathe in and out, releasing the stress and worries as we recall the peace that God provides as he calms the storms of life. Let God in, and he will work it all out for you. "In peace, I will both lie down and sleep; for you alone, o Lord, make me dwell in safety." **(Psalms 4:8)**

We have hope in him because he is all that we truly need. Because we aren't to be anxious about anything, "Do not be anxious about anything, but in everything by prayer and supplication with Thanksgiving let your requests be made known to God." **(Phillippians 4:6).**

Once we are confident in knowing we trust him, he will provide, he will deliver and in him we are safe. We know this because he's done this for us, and if you take a look at your life and story, you may see him showing up for you as well. Therefore, we have the peace that will keep us: "And the peace of God, which surpasses all understanding, will guard your hearts and your minds in Christ Jesus." **(Philippians 4:7)**

God's Peace surpasses all the things we don't get because he is our peace, and that is why we can come to him about anything. He is the answer, but we get used to getting anxious and becoming afraid of what may happen because of our current situation. Suppose we keep our eyes on Jesus, like when the Apostle Peter was walking on water and didn't take his eyes off of Christ when the wind came, and he got scared of sinking into the water.

He would've walked all across that water, meeting his maker, watching his faith be activated and gaining a peace that cannot be moved no matter what the situation is.

We have to hold on to God's promise he made to us, keeping our eyes on him, knowing that he will see us through our lowest situations and when we experience his peace, we are rest assured that everything is going to be alright.

Let's connect: It wasn't until I got older that I realized how important peace was to me. I stopped worrying so much and allowing fear to take control, and I gave it to God and watched him take care of me.

Let's talk about it:

Are you someone who struggles with worrying?

How do you cope during those times?

Have you ever experienced God's peace?

What are some things you can practice now to be more at peace?

Protecting our lives, God gave us

＊＋●＋＊

"The name of the Lord is a strong tower; the righteous man runs into it and is safe" **(Proverbs 18:10)**

The Lord says, "Fear not, for I am with you; be not dismayed, for I am your God; I will strengthen you, I will help you, I will uphold you with my righteous right hand." **(Isaiah 41:10)**

God loves us so much, and he created us for his purpose and his alone. It is important that we take precautions to ensure that we take very good care of ourselves.

We have to entrust our lives to the one who can ensure our safety and full care. We know that God has our best interest at heart.

We can count on him that once our lives are in his hands, we'll be taken care of in return. We must remain mindful and hopeful that we do our due diligence to maintain a safe and healthy lifestyle around us. We know the things we ought to do and the things we shouldn't to make sure we are on the right track in our lives. If we don't, it is good to gain the knowledge, understanding, and wisdom to know what to do.

We can have confidence in this fact that "Even to your old age I am he, and to gray hairs I will carry you. I have made, and will bear; I will carry and will save" **(Isaiah 46:4)**

I know that during the time the world was affected and impacted by COVID-19, it changed a lot of things and the way we conducted ourselves, and we had to be very careful as this disease came to kill, steal, and destroy lives, and it already has.

There were so many rules and restraints set out during this pandemic that was very frustrating but was for us to be safe, and also prevent the spread of the disease as well. Like sanitizing our hands, social distancing, and wearing masks that were hard to breathe in, we also had to get the vaccination so that our chances of getting COVID-19 could be lessened.

From the beginning of time, we see the great vision and plan God manifested by creating us. We have to put our trust and faith in him, knowing that whatever we face in life, he will see us through.

We know the journey we took, even though we may have been frustrated with the protocols placed during COVID-19, was given for our safety and protection. We can see the benefits of doing so, as David says in **Psalms 17:8, David** says, "Keep me as the apple of your eye; hide me in the shadow of your wings."

Once we put our trust in who God is to us, we can depend on him to deliver us through every disaster or storm we may face in life. There isn't anything that God can't do; we just have to believe that once we pray and look for him during our times of need, he'll come through as he did for me, and you can rest assured that he can do the same for you as well.

Pray that the Lord will cover us with his blood, which is holy, pure and able to keep us. Not only that, but we rejoice in our sufferings. Knowing that suffering produces endurance, and endurance produces character, and character produces hope." **(Romans 5:3-4)**

"Blessed is he who has regard for the weak; the Lord delivers him in times of trouble. The LORD will protect him and preserve his life; he will bless him in the land and not surrender him to the desire of his foes. The Lord sustains him on his sickbed; in his illness, you restore him to full health." **(Psalm 41:1)**

"He gives power to the faint, and to him who has no might, he increases strength. Even youths shall faint and be weary, and young men shall fall exhausted, but they who wait for the LORD shall renew their strength; they shall mount up with wings like eagles; they shall run and not be weary; they shall walk and not faint." **(Isaiah 40:29-31)**

Let's connect: My favorite hymn is Blessed Assurance. It is so reassuring to know that Jesus is mine simply because I chose to have fellowship with him. My life belongs to him, and I am safe because I can always depend on him to protect me.

Let's talk about it:

In what ways have you seen God's protection over your life?

During COVID-19 did you pray more during this time for God to keep you and your family?

Has your understanding of God become clearer to you?

Where are some areas in your life today, you'd like God to manifest himself?

Loving our neighbor
(being mindful of others)

"This is my commandment, that you love one another as I have loved you. **(John 15:12)**

With everything we have to face in life, we have a lot going on. How do we manage it all as we witness the stress of the world during the pandemic? And the frustration many had to face with sickness, job loss, losing loved ones, fewer social events, and so much more.

There will be times of despair, loss, grief, anger, and even disbelief. However, throughout all of these, we have to be mindful not only of ourselves but also of others because we have to all live in this world together, getting along and pulling through.

I remember my own experience during the pandemic was one of great isolation. You could no longer greet your neighbor for fear of catching the sickness or hold the door due to the germs; eye contact was scary because it was as if you might catch COVID-19 with just a look. So, there was rarely any eye contact at all.

God wants us to love him first because love is an act, not a mere feeling. When we love God, we love what and who he loves. **James 2:8** states, "If you really fulfill the royal law according to the scripture, "You shall love your neighbor as yourself," You are doing well."

" Let love be genuine. Abhor what is evil; hold fast to what is good."

(**Romans 12:9**)

Relationships are great connections to have because if we can live together in harmony we can do great work together. When we love ourselves, we love others the same way we do. We wouldn't want to be rude to someone who did nothing to you only because we are frustrated.

However, you realize that your frustration doesn't have anything to do with this person and out of love, you'd find a solution. Who knows, sometimes that person can hold your hand with you, empathize with your frustration and help you find a solution.

God desires good relationships to be made here while we are all on earth. We are to love one another, and out of this love for God, we can love others just the same. Love can do effective change, which we need during the ups and downs of life.

Let's connect:

I used to think that my neighbor was the person who lived next door to me, but I learned that everyone we interact with is our neighbor. How we interact with each other matters, and it is good to start now.

Let's talk about it:

Did you have a good experience with others during the pandemic?

What were your thoughts on loving your neighbor before?

How can God help you with your relationships with others?

Do you treat others the way you'd like to be treated?

How to deal with conflicting situations

It isn't easy at times, and the Lord knows that we've been through some things, especially when we can all relate to the tragic virus that took over the entire world.

For me, having faith in God brought me and my family through. The government did put in strict measures, which I understand wasn't easy for us all to cope with, but it was necessary until we got this virus controlled. Now, we see the effect this had on our regained sense of freedom.

However, for some, it was family; for others, it could be just staying healthy and keeping in touch with family and friends via social platforms to still connect on video chat or calling. How does God want us to deal with conflicting situations? Should we panic, have fear, or get frantic because we don't know the outcomes?

I find that we are in a time where we want everything to be resolved quickly. We put our food in the Microwave or want to get food quickly at the drive-thru because we are hungry and need to eat right now. So, we sometimes don't have the patience to wait for things to be resolved.

It is fair to call it what it is because it can be tough, and if it is, that's true. Do we believe in who God says he is to us? Who is God to you? The Bible shows us so many names of God, but in your life, even before COVID-19, who did God represent to you?

Like some of God's names are "Abba Father, or Immanuel, "God is with us. I AM, and to name a few more, we have Jehovah Rapha, which means "The Lord who heals." he declares to you, "Behold, I will bring to it health and healing, and I will heal them and reveal to them an abundance of prosperity and security." **(Jeremiah 33:6)**

Who does God represent in your life? Is he your healer, deliverer, the God you depend on to provide for you as he has? When you know who he is to you, then he becomes this sustaining power in your life continually. If you have a sickness in your life, such as COVID-19, you are calling on your God, the healer, and this is what he is going to reassure you with. So, then, you are praying these things over your life: "Heal me, O Lord, and I shall be healed; save me, and I shall be saved for you are my praise" **(Jeremiah 17:14).**

If he is your provider, because you first have to believe and have faith in him being your provider, you speak this over your life: "And my God will supply every need of yours according to his riches in glory in Christ Jesus." **(Phillippians 4:19).**

Once we put all of our matters to God, we are safe to know that he can see us through. We can pray and trust in his goodness and mercy to bring us through every situation. There isn't anything too hard for God, nor too big or too small, he can't fix. We have to see this for ourselves in what we choose to believe because, in **John 14:27,** he says, "Peace I leave with you; my peace I give to you. Not as the world gives do I give to you. Let not your hearts be troubled, neither let them be afraid."

How we respond to our situations is what really matters the most, and once we take those steps in faith, we begin to see him work in our lives; we then have this blessed assurance.

"A Psalms of David. The Lord is my shepherd; I shall not want. He makes me lie down in green pastures. He leads me beside still waters. He restores my soul. He leads me in paths of righteousness for his name's sake. Even though I walk through the valley of the shadow of death, I will fear no evil, for you are with me; your rod and your staff, they comfort me. **(Psalm 23: 1-5).**

I couldn't imagine a life of struggle and strife and not having faith to help me make it through. We have to rely on something higher than ourselves because we need strength beyond our own, grace to bring us through, and mercy to save us.

The biggest thing to depend on is having a dependable God. We have too many references to the testimonies of God's goodness. There is no greater love than what God has to offer to help us live this life now and forevermore.

Let's Connect: Who likes conflict or situations that cause so much stress? We can focus on the solution; there is one for every problem. God knows them all.

Let's talk about it:

What do you normally do when faced with conflict?

Do you activate your faith during those times by doing what?

Can you reflect on a situation you had and how God brought you through it?

Is there a conflict or situation you'd like God to help you through? What specific outcome would you like to ask for?

Trusting God when it doesn't always look good

When I look up the word trust in the Dictionary, it states that it means "Confidence in or reliance on some person or quality." It can also mean reliability because a person should be reliable if you will depend on them.

Trust is so important today. I find it so hard to trust people these days. With so many scams and crooks out there, and sometimes, it's not even the strangers you have to worry about; it can be family and friends you cannot trust either.

God states that he isn't like man. He is God of integrity, and what he says, he is going to do he will stand on his word and do it. He has to be honest because he is true. He has to be someone reliable because he will never lie. "God is not man, that he should lie, or a son of man, that he should change his mind. Has he said, and will he not do it? Or has he spoken, and will he not fulfill it?" **(Numbers 23:19)**

We are going to have up-and-down days and seasons in our lives where we wonder, "What is up, God?" We may think that, given what we are experiencing, it is hard to believe God is not with us, but he is nearer than we think.

I remember a time in my life when I was experiencing very little change. It felt like I was sailing on a boat for a very long time, getting weary of the long journey and wanting to reach my final destination. I felt like God wasn't there, so one night, I prayed, "Lord, are you here?" As I was about to go to sleep, I heard what sounded like a crash outside.

When I looked, I saw my car being hit by another driver who was reversing. It looked staged, but my adrenaline spiked, and I ran down the stairs before the driver could even think about doing a hit-and-run. I put on a pair of shoes, still wearing my pajamas, and rushed out the door.

I don't know why I thought I could run like an Olympic track runner. My gosh! My mind made me think I could do anything at that moment. As I was getting ready to run after this driver, I heard a stranger tell me, "Don't worry, we got this recorded on video." He stated that he and another guy caught all the action on tape and were just here visiting and seeing this happening.

I was furious, but look at God - he showed up to answer my prayer. I actually met him there because he was already getting everything set up. So, when I arrived, he said, "My child, of course I am here. Do you trust me now?" I sure do, Lord.

God helped us out. We got the report made, and it went through successfully. God sorted everything out, and our car got fixed.

Trusting God is hard when we are looking at the situations we face and we don't know what God is going to do or if he will do anything at all. So we begin to think a lot or wonder what we are going to do, but when we look to the Lord, we can trust him because we know that in every situation we take to him, he is able to come through for us. Like he did for me, he showed up when I just needed some more faith. It is alright to speak out and say I need some more faith because he can help us strengthen our belief in him some more. "The apostles said to the Lord, "Increase our faith!" **(Luke 17:5)**

Once we remind ourselves who God is in our life, we can only but have his peace, which covers and guides us: "You keep him in perfect peace whose mind is stayed on you, because he trusts in you. Trust in the Lord forever, for the Lord God is an everlasting rock." **(Isaiah 26:3-4)**

Let's Connect: Trust is crucial in relationships, as it is the glue that holds everything together. We need to trust in who God is because we know he will do what he says he will do. We have no doubt in him.

Let's talk about it:

How important is trust in a relationship for you?

When things aren't looking up, do you have doubts that God will come through for you?

Was there any time in your life when you needed to ask God for more faith?

Do you trust God, and if so, why?

Why do sickness, trials and tribulations come?

There are many reasons why sickness has entered our world, but I believe the greatest reason is sin. "Afterward, Jesus found him in the temple and said to him, "See, you are well! Sin no more, that nothing worse may happen to you." **(John 5:14)** Sin destroys our inner man, which is our spirit, which is a very vital part of our being.

"We have all become like one who is unclean, and all our righteous deeds are like a dirty garment. We all fade like a leaf, and our iniquities, like the wind, take us away." **(Isaiah 64:6).** The spirit needs an able body, mind, and soul to strive in. Pollution and what we consume as food, drink, and drugs. Those contribute to the body getting ill.

However, a thought just passed my mind as I wrote this, but sorrow and the stress of life are also big concerns. "He heals the brokenhearted and binds up their wounds." **(Psalm 147:3)**

"He will wipe away every tear from their eyes, and death shall be no more, neither shall there be mourning, nor crying, nor pain anymore, for the former things have passed away." **(Revelation 21:4)**

"Count it all joy, my brothers, when you meet trials of various kinds, for you know that the testing of your faith produces steadfastness. And let steadfastness have its full effect, that you may be perfect and complete, lacking in nothing" **(James 1:2-3)**

"Is anyone among you sick? Let him call for the elders of the church, and let them pray over him, anointing him with oil in the name of the Lord. And the prayer of faith will save the one who is sick, and the Lord will raise him up And if he has committed sins, he will be forgiven." **(James 5:14-15)**

Joy is medicine to the bones.

"A joyful heart is good medicine, but a crushed spirit dries up the bones." **(Proverbs 17:22)**

I believe there is a significant reason why God does not want us to worry, hold no grudges, or be bitter inside. These intense feelings can have an effect on our bodies, causing an imbalance within us. We must bring all of our heavy burdens before him. We can start with love and joy, which results in a happy state that is good for our bones.

I know it is easier said than done, but Christ can help us get through anything.

He says in **John 16:33,** "I have said these things to you, that in me you may have peace. In the world you will have tribulation. But take heart; I have overcome the world."

There was a song we used to sing in church where it said, "When trouble is in your life, sing praises, and sing praises with understanding. Because God is our king over all the earth."

I love listening to some good, uplifting, and positive music to keep my perspectives on God enriched and remain in high vibrations. It takes us away to a place where we can take our focus on what we are going through and get connected with God.

We must stay focused and pray, look over scriptures on what God says about sickness and going through trials and tribulations and speak those things into our lives. God is true to his word, and you speak those in your life and, believe in God and watch him do wonders for you.

There was a story in the Bible that demonstrated that this man was blind. It was not that he had sinned and done something very bad to become blind, but it was to demonstrate God's miraculous power.

"Many are the afflictions of the righteous, but the Lord delivers him out of them all." **(Psalm 34:19)**

"As he passed by, he saw a man blind from birth." And his disciples asked him, "Rabbi, who sinned, this man or his parents, that he was born blind?" Jesus answered, "It was not that this man sinned, or his parents, but that the works of God might be displayed in him. **(John 9:1-7)**

We can see that some things happen in our lives for God's power to manifest in our lives. Then we can say that he was our healer, our deliver, refuge, strength and peace.

Let's Connect:

What a joy to know that all we face, God's got us. Trials have nothing on us because we shall win. We already have won battles of our own.

Let's talk about it.

What are some of the trials and tribulations you've been through?

Have you reflected on them and seen God's strength getting you through?

Before God, how were you handling those hardships?

Now, do you see a significant difference with God involved?

How to experience peace, love, and Joy during crisis

—◆●◆—

"Now may the Lord of peace himself give you peace at all times in every way. The Lord be with you all." **(2 Thessalonians 3:16)**

It is good to know that throughout all that we've been through and are going through right now. We have a God who cares about us and wants us to experience peace and love, as well as the joy only he can give us. Because best of all, he is all of these which we seek. We have to put our faith in Him, trust him with all of our lives, and allow him to see us through.

As I became older and went through a life of chaos, at times, it was hard to experience the peace that the world offers. Like that chocolate you indulge in after a long stressful day, but only that it is consumed so fast and doesn't satisfy the deep longing for rest I truly need.

I used to want another and then another chocolate until I realized it was too much. "Peace, I leave with you; the peace I give to you. Not as the world gives do I give to you. Let not your hearts be troubled, neither let them be afraid." **(John 14:27).**

I began to notice God's peace in my life when very drastic situations that would normally be big problems for me became still.

When all the drama ended, and my circle became so small that it was left with just me and the Lord, I yearned for this peace and was very grateful I was able to experience it in those seasons. God has shown me that I can trust him because whatever I go through, he will be right there. "He promises to never leave or forsake me."

"May the Lord give strength to his people!!! May the Lord bless his people with peace!" **(Psalm 29:11)**

I chose to be peaceful, to have joy and love where things no longer bother me like before. A profound truth I now understand much more is to live one day at a time. Trust me! There is power in just living right now and not thinking about the worries of tomorrow. Let tomorrow figure out itself it's a new day with something different you can handle as it comes.

A lot of what worries us are the affairs of life: bills, relationships, work, life, and finding harmony between all things. We have a God who knows it all, the beginning, middle, and end of all things. God has shown me time and time again that I am safe in him, as he has brought me through so many difficult times, and I am here to speak of his goodness today.

We carry a lot of the burdens of yesterday, such as our past and what we went through, which are leaving us broken and so wounded we cannot look past the hurt and pain. However, God wants to take our wounds and help us let it all go. We won't excuse what we went through as nothing, but we must take hold of the love, joy, and peace God can give us to live well. To do better today and for our future.

Personally, for me, I looked for love in my younger days in all the wrong places. When I experienced the Love of God, I was astonished that he'd actually love me. I was ashamed of all the things I had done when I didn't know better, but he embraced me, gave me my purpose, and told me who I was. I finally found someone who wanted me, I was accepted and belonged and became a citizen of his Kingdom. He had so many great things to say to me. I was surprised, but I can receive them today because I believe him. You can speak those things to yourself as well and say this, I am loved, I am accepted, I am worthy of his peace, and capable of living in his joy and receiving his love.

Just seeing the overwhelming experience, we had as I watched the whole world go through COVID it was a scary experience, because any little mistake could cost you your life. You had to make sure you followed all the protocols given to stay in line.

It was a big test for all of us, but when we see what God has saved us from, we surely can see how much he truly loves us. Because, after all, we love him because he first sought out his love for us. "We love because he first loved us." **(1 John 4:19).**

Look over your life, the good, the bad, and the ugly moments, and now look at you at this present moment. Take in those deep breaths in and out, slowly, and see God's love in your life. It is a choice you have to make to believe that you see God in your life, showing you how much he loves you.

"So we have to come to know and to believe the love that God has for us. God is love, and whoever abides in love abides in God, and God abides in him." **(1 John 4:16).** That is exactly why we have to put our faith in God, give him our life and experience all that Christ has for us.

We need the Holy Spirit, who can lead us through all truth in our specific time and need.

The holy spirit is like a friend who will walk with you in the good and bad times. He won't run when things get hard. Like that friend who sticketh closer than his brother: He teaches you what he knows and guides you through everything. Helps you by praying for you when you don't know what to pray for. He is constant, loyal, and so close to us. He comforts us and encourages us, keeping us motivated and powerful to be who we were created to be.

We'd look crazy, right? To be so joyful in moments of crisis, but it is good when it is in the Lord. I just love joy. It is more than just a smile on its face. It is the reason to have life and live it abundantly in Christ. God is so joyful and loves to share this with us all. We often feel so condemned, saddened by grief, and overtaken by strife and regrets. We miss out on experiencing this great joy.

Numerous situations we've been through have caused us to feel defeated. We all can relate to COVID-19 and what we experienced. However, when we review what we've gone through, we can say, "We are still alive, we have great health; some of us still have a job throughout the ordeal; we got COVID-19 and were healed" (Praise the Lord).

Now, my heart goes out to all those who weren't as fortunate. Look up and keep on seeking the Lord, looking towards faith in him to bring you out and restore his peace, love, and joy back into your life. I know many didn't survive the ordeal we experienced, but live this life for your loved ones, holding to their memories and finding true purpose for living your life.

Let's connect: If I were asked which one would be the most important for me between Peace, Love and Joy. I would want to say all three are needed, but the most important one is love, because everything comes from love.

Let's talk about it:

Out of the three, peace, love, and joy. Which one do you deem most important and why?

How did God express his love, joy, and peace in your life?

How do you demonstrate love to others?

Do you have any challenges in your life keeping you from experiencing peace, love, or joy?

How to get the abundance of life God has for us

—◆●◆—

"The thief comes only to steal and kill and destroy. I come that they may have life and have it abundantly **(John 10:10)**

The word of God states, "But seek first the kingdom of God and his righteousness, and all these things will be added to you." **(Matthew 6:33)**

God is abundant in himself because he has much to give us. He can never run out or be short of anything if we lack strength, love, faith, mercy, or grace. We get his abundance because if we live a life excluding God, we aren't living; we exist. We begin to live when we know who we are and become the person fulfilling our calling or destiny.

Once we go through the journey and gain the knowledge, we know how important God is in our daily lives. We understand that our lives are more valuable, purposeful, and prosperous than silver and gold.

Our choices in life hold significance to both God and ourselves. We've been through so much in this lifetime, and we shouldn't have to face it all alone.

God desires to be integrated into every aspect of our lives. By welcoming him, we open ourselves to his abundant blessings. Including Him in our daily routines is crucial to ensure we receive the necessary support to navigate through life's challenging, sometimes overwhelming, and disheartening moments.

God blesses us with faith, hope, love, and peace. He is wise, and we can trust him to lead us safely through everything. God has given each of us the gift of life so that we can live and live it purposely with him. He has a plan for each of us to fulfill his will so that we may all be part of his abundant inheritance.

He calls all of his to be reconciled to a relationship we can have with him again. This is through his son, Jesus Christ, who can give us all the abundant life we need. He's got so much of himself for everyone, so you can always count on him.

Let's connect: I love to have life, and having life in Christ has been the greatest decision of my life. Just knowing that I don't just have life, but abundant living—now that's amazing!!!!!

Let's talk about it:

What was your understanding of abundance before?

Are you currently living an abundant life? If so, what does that look like?

Since God desires us to reconcile with him through his son Jesus, what are the next steps you'd like to take to allow this to happen?

What help do you need to seek God for?

Gratitude is our new attitude

What is Gratitude? The dictionary defines it as "the act of being grateful." It stands for appreciation and thankfulness.

What are we grateful for or thankful to God for, and how do we demonstrate our gratefulness to him?

We can say thank you for many things we can think of. One of the greatest things I would begin with is being grateful for life. If I weren't here, I wouldn't be able to speak of this, so therefore, I am happy that I can thank God for living and having the breath of life. "For the grave cannot praise thee, death cannot celebrate thee: They that go down into the pit cannot hope for thy truth. The living, the living, he shall praise thee, as I do this day: The father to the children shall make known thy truth." **(Isaiah 38:18-20 KJV)**

What makes us sometimes feel unappreciated is the hardship we often go through; we have too many heartbreaks and disappointments where we know we exist but are not entirely living to our full potential. Therefore, we don't express much gratitude. We don't feel appreciated in life, so we come with heavy hearts to God. The word says in **1 Thessalonians 5:16-18** that we should "Rejoice always, pray without ceasing, give thanks in all circumstances; for this is the will of God in Christ Jesus for you."

79

When we are downcast and hurting, we don't always feel like rejoicing, but we are directed here to rejoice, not sometimes or when we want, but always. Every single time we face difficulties, we are to rejoice. God knows us so well, as he is our maker, and studies us so closely to understand our mind, what we do, why we do it, and to know us so deeply.

These instructions are given to us wisely because in sin comes so much pain, but the spirit comes with the fruits of the spirit, such as Love, Joy, Peace, Patience, Kindness, Goodness, Faithfulness, Gentleness, and Self-control under the guidance of the Holy Spirit.

Joy is so sweet to the soul because it can help us get through the highest mountain we have to climb and the deepest valley we have to cross. "Count it all joy, my brothers, when you meet trials of various kinds." (James 1:2).

So, we can count it all joy when we know who we are coming to with our situations and problems. We wouldn't go to the doctor whom we heard has a track record of doing wrong things, causing harm and even death to others.

We wouldn't go to the bank that takes from you instead of giving you solutions when you are in need, nor would we go to the food bank that tells us that you have to have money when you are poor and hungry. The answer would surely be No!

However, if we go to Jesus, we know he can be all these things for us and more. So when situations arise, we are excited to see him come through again.

There he goes, getting another home run time and time again, just scoring big time in your life. When you review your life and see all the things you've overcome, and you see God did this, you have a new attitude, and it looks like gratitude.

Because we don't want our kids to get things we work so hard for and say they are thankful, but then we see them lying around, broken just after we bought them, or not even being used when they asked for them. We need to see gratitude.

They can do this by taking good care of the things we get for them and do for them. The best way to do this is by listening to us and following the rules at home and everywhere they go, doing their chores without us having to constantly remind them. Be respectful in and out of the home. That is the attitude we need from them.

God, being our father, is similar. We can be thankful, but what we do shows our gratitude towards him. Because words are simple, they are the beginning of things. We must complete them with our actions because we know "Actions speak louder than words." So, when we want to demonstrate our gratitude to God, we must ensure our lives say this.

Bills are due, and we come to God all happy, saying Lord, here's another problem for you to solve, and I know, Lord, you are about to come through. Because if you did it before, you can surely do it again, and your word says, "And my God will supply every need of yours according to his riches in glory in Christ Jesus." **(Phillippians 4:19).** We come to God being thankful because we know what he is capable of doing and using what we learn from our own experiences and what others have gone through we know he is the same God then and now. "Jesus Christ is the same yesterday and today and forever." **(Hebrews 13:8)**

So, we can trust that he is dependable and consistent in his nature and character.

Let's look at this story, which demonstrates the act of gratitude.

"On the way to Jerusalem he was passing along between Samaria and Galilee. And as he entered a village, he was met by ten lepers, who stood at a distance and lifted up their voices, saying, "Jesus, Master, have mercy on us."

When he saw them, he said to them, "Go and show yourselves to the priests." And as they went, they were cleansed. Then one of them, when we saw that he was healed, turned back, praising God with a loud voice, and he fell on his face at Jesus' feet, giving him thanks. Now, he was a Samaritan.

Then Jesus answered, "Were not ten cleansed? Where are the nine? Was no one found to return and give praise to God except this foreigner?" And he said to him, "Rise and go your way; your faith has made you well." **(Luke 17:11-19)**

We see a man who was oppressed by the disease of Leprosy. Who cried out to the one he believed in who could have mercy on him. "Jesus, Master, have mercy on us." Jesus used one word, "Go," and sent them away to show the priests that he had cleansed them. Did all of them show their gratefulness to God? Only one turned back as he followed his command to go to the priest.

He could have just taken his healing and gone on his way, but he came back to give praise, and it states, "Praising God with a loud voice" and also fell on his face at Jesus' feet, giving him thanks. He showed that he was grateful, and the others just took their healing, not pouring it back into the one who gave it to them. He let God know with his actions that he deserved the praise to know that he was truly thankful for giving him back his life.

We must remember to live our lives demonstrating this gratitude. After all, we are still here to do it and take the time to see him work wonders in your own life. We can read everyone's story cause it's easier to go through, but we mustn't be afraid to go over our own lives.

God has been good, and with a loud voice, we say, "Thank you, Lord." Now, "rise and go your way; your faith has made you well."

Let's connect:

The first thing I love to do when I wake up in the morning is thank God for life. Just getting another day lets me know I am still running my race, and it's time to finish my work. Hallelujah

Let's talk about it:

Did the story of the leper who came back to praise the Lord show you how important being grateful is to God?

How do you demonstrate gratefulness to God?

What are some ways you can start showing gratitude to God and others around you?

Make a list of all the things you are grateful for, and thank God for them.

Be blessed, and blessings flow to others

"Blessed are the poor in spirit, for theirs is the kingdom of heaven. "Blessed are those who mourn, for they shall be comforted. "Blessed are the meek, for they shall inherit the earth. "Blessed are those who hunger and thirst for righteousness, for they shall be satisfied. "Blessed are the merciful, for they shall receive mercy." **(Matthew 5:3-7).**

Once we are blessed by God, we can see that we will indeed be covered and given what we rightfully deserve in return. If God blesses us, being poor in spirit, we will gain the Kingdom of heaven. If we are mourning, we are guaranteed to be comforted. If we live for the will of God, we will indeed be blessed.

His blessing is far beyond what the eyes can only see because we see all these big and flashy things and associate those as blessings from God. There is simply more to life that God wants to offer us.

More significant than the material things this world can offer, I love nice things myself, but I want to know that if I have a pure heart, I will be closer to God to see his goodness. That kind of relationship is deep and guarantees much more success.

But he said, "Blessed rather are those who hear the word of God and keep it! **(Luke 11:28).**

We are blessed when God approves of our lives, when we live up to his laws and live them out every day. **Psalms 1: 1-3** demonstrates how you ought to be blessed and how to remain. "Blessed is the man who walks not in the counsel of the wicked, nor stands in the way of sinners, nor sits in the seat of scoffers, but his delight is in the law of the Lord, and on his law he meditates day and night. He is like a tree planted by streams of water that yields its fruit in its season, and its leaf does not wither. In all that he does, he prospers."

Therefore, to be blessed, we cannot take counsel from the wicked simply because they would lead us astray and cause us to sin against God. We'll do the wrong things, which won't keep God happy in us. We don't stand or be around people who want to sin because you cannot have two masters; you'll have to choose which one you'd like to follow. Being around sinners may entice you to follow their ways. You don't sit with those people who are scoffers.

"Scoffer" is the name of the arrogant, haughty man who acts with arrogant pride." **(Proverbs 21:24).** You wouldn't want to sit with someone who has arrogant pride, especially when it comes to the things of God. They will discourage you from walking right.

So, we should delight in the law of the Lord. When we delight in his laws, we find it enjoyable to follow them; we want to do them because they are good for us.

How did we feel when we were given the law to wear masks during COVID-19, and we were so grumpy or disappointed to wear them? Trust me, I know those masks were unbearable, and we could hardly breathe, but we know this rule was set for our own good. I'm glad we followed through because we now see the results weren't so bad after all. If we did this law with happiness and being delightful with its insightful instructions, we'd go through it more easily.

We also have to meditate on his law day and night. We have to go over it all day to make sure we remember it and understand it.

Then, we see the picture of a tree planted by streams of water getting the nourishment it requires to survive. The best thing is that it will yield its fruit in its season. This isn't a barren tree; it will do what it's supposed to do in its season, and it won't get old and wither away.

Aging doesn't affect this blessed man or woman of God because they are walking in God's victory, living fully for him. The promise is that you follow all the do's and don'ts of his command, and you are walking aligned with God.

The good thing is that once we are blessed and receive God's goodness, why wouldn't we want to share this with others? It doesn't always have to be in the form of money, but it can be how we treat our neighbors. We must manifest the fruits of the spirit when we say we are "Children of God."

There will be moments we'll have to showcase that we live the laws of God, and those laws will manifest themselves when it is time to apply them to your life and others. When we are blessed, we just want to pour that love and goodness into others. Sharing our joy as others may be experiencing sorrow. We can give love to others who are facing hate every day. We can showcase peace to others because they've been fighting so much, and they need kindness because they've been bullied for as long as they can remember. They need goodness because they only receive terrible things in their life. You don't know who you may meet and what they need to feel a glimpse of hope that someone cares.

It is our duty as people of God to demonstrate his kingdom here on earth because that is the plan that we'd all be able to live in eternity with God and his chosen people forever and ever. Amen. So, when do we want to demonstrate this? When Christ returns, it will be too late as you don't have much time to fix all your wrongs at that time. Do it now, that you have the chance.

Let us demonstrate faithfulness to one another because there are those who have been abandoned by many and cannot trust. Be gentle in dealing with situations or with people you don't know. Because how you treat them could be where they have a breaking point and are damaged beyond repair. Be very careful how we are to ourselves as we need wholeness to give to others. Make sure you remember yourself and that you also need this for yourself as well.

Lastly, we want to demonstrate self-control guided by the Holy Spirit so we can give others the chance of redemption and grace. We remember how many times God could have sent that flood our way time and time again because humanity keeps on sinning, but his promise stands, and he won't ever go against his word. He promised he wouldn't do this, and it is true.

We live in this world together until Christ returns. Why can't we change our vision from individualism to collectively so that everyone is a blessed people of God? We know what we'll receive back as he says, "In all that he does, he prospers" **(Psalms 1 :3).** Let's be a people who want all to prosper because the world would be a much better place for that.

Let's Connect: Let God do his work through us so that we can see this happen, and everyone will be blessed together. I love the sound of this already!! It will be a time of Jubilee.

Let's talk about it:

What does being blessed look like to you?

Can you use the illustration of the tree to become blessed by God?

How can you incorporate God in your blessings?

Did you see yourself as a blessed person before? If not. How come?

Love is the answer

What is Love? Where does this feeling come from?

It states in **John 3:16**, "For God so loved the world, that he gave his only Son, that whoever believes in him should not perish but have eternal life."

I looked this up in the dictionary to see what it means, and it states, "A deep caring for the existence of another" or "A profound and caring affection towards someone."

I used to think love was a feeling, but I began to understand that if we followed that sentiment, I would love you today and not tomorrow. Because feelings go up and down, I saw it as an act you give to another.

Like I remember when I was affected by COVID, and when I wasn't feeling well, my other family members weren't as well. However, even though they weren't their best, they'd still come and help me by bringing me juice or checking up to see if I was alright.

We see that God did the most significant act of love by giving us something so precious and dear to him, but our knowing now is also very precious to us because we know the significance of what Jesus did for us by dying on the cross for our sins.

God represents Love, and he has so much love for all of humanity. If it was simply a feeling and he just said he loved us, but we never received redemption with Christ's sacrifice, how'd we know this love? That is the feeling, but he went above and beyond all we could ask or think.

We have to have God's love because we still need to learn the right way to love. We get so many misconceptions of what love is from the things we watch and the music we listen to. When you realize relationships cannot just survive off of mere feelings but actual work. They need things to be done, and each role needs to be fulfilled, or else there is a lack.

Love is truly the answer because we can have faith and hope, but love is the greatest of them all. "So now faith, hope, and love abide, these three; but the greatest of these is love." (**1 Corinthians 13:13**)

I just love to love it is such a beautiful aspect of life, especially to experience God's love. When I met his love, I was mesmerized because he took me in his wings and taught me so many things about life, myself and who he is. That is why he can be a jealous God at times.

Why shouldn't he feel angry or disappointed after creating humanity, breathing life into us, and giving us his spirit, only for us to turn to other gods or choose to live in sin? How is this supposed to make him feel? We are his great masterpiece; he was proud of what he created.

Every time I look back at where he brought me from, I can see his love. When I was lying sick on my sickbed, he was there, and with the power of his holy Spirit, he healed me. He truly represents love to me because he has shown it to me too many times.

We have to demonstrate this love by receiving God's love for ourselves, and then we can give it to others. Fill your cup so it can run over for another.

"For there is no respect of persons with God" (**Romans 2:11**).

So that means he isn't going to be fair to a set of people just based on who they are. If you are the president of this world, it isn't the same thing when you get to the kingdom of God. You will be known by your name and your deeds, so make sure that your name speaks precedence of who you say you are.

If we want others to know we are truly one of God's disciples we have to show forth this through our actions.

"A new commandment I give to you, that you love one another: just as I have loved you, you also are to love one another. By this, all people will know what you are, my disciples, if you have love for one another" (**John 13:34-35**).

Once we have God's love in our hearts and we live by the spirit of his truth and love we can manifest this because there is an order to how we are to love. "Jesus answered, "The most important is, 'Hear, O Israel: The Lord our God, the Lord is one. And you shall love the Lord your God with all your heart and with all your soul and with all your mind and with all your strength.' The second is this: 'You shall love your neighbor as yourself.' There is no other commandment greater than these." (**Mark 12:29-31**)

It isn't always easy to show love, but I learned, and it was told to me that "love is much more powerful when it's hardest to do." I believe in this because it's easy to love another when they are doing right by you. However, in their pride and ignorance, they can get the "I don't know about this love," but we know we have to pray for them and that love cannot be turned off.

Because **1 Corinthians 13:4-8** it gives us some instructions when our love is being challenged. It says;

"Love is patient and kind; love does not envy or boast; it is not arrogant or rude. It does not insist on its own way; it is not irritable or resentful; it does not rejoice at wrongdoing but rejoices with the truth. Love bears all things, believes all things, hopes all things, endures all things. Love never ends. As for prophecies, they will pass away; as for tongues, they will cease; as for knowledge, it will pass away."

We can remember this when we are being tested to go against what is right and give in to our sinful nature, wanting to take revenge on those who hurt us. We must try our best to stay true to our beliefs and not lose our values to go down to their level. It costs us too much to lose our high stance on life, and how we respond to situations is truly important.

After all, "Let all that you do be done in love" **(1 Corinthians 16:14).**

Let's connect: One of the greatest songs I heard about Jesus' love was "Jesus loves the little children, all the children of the world. Red and yellow, black and white, we are precious in his sight. Jesus loves the little children of the world."

Let's talk about it:

What did you think love was before reading this chapter?

What are your thoughts on how God demonstrated his love for you?

Do you doubt God's love for you? Write a journal entry addressing what is preventing you from fully experiencing or accepting His love.

What does love look like to you?

Faith in times of need

◄◄◦◦◦►►

"And without faith, it is impossible to please him, for whoever would draw near to God must believe that he exists and that he rewards those who seek him." **(Hebrews 11:6)**

I always hear this said to me, "Do you believe?" as if you can close your eyes and think and say, "Yes, I do believe. How did I come to believe in Jesus? Now, that is a remarkable story because some may think as a child, when I had to go to church, I was forced to believe or that what I saw on TV made me follow a trend, and I wanted to belong, so I joined. Or I was lost and had no idea, so I simply chose to have faith in Jesus.

When it all began, I decided that this was the truth for my life. I wanted to take this journey because of its amazing truth, its deliverance, its hope, and also God's love for me.

My faith began when I saw the mess—I saw myself transparent in front of God—when I saw the stain of sins and heard of a Man who could wash all my sins away. I would cry about the things I've done and feel so much shame and guilt that when I heard about the Lord, I answered his call when he came for me.

In those days, I was big on going to parties because I loved to dance, so I wasn't ready to put away my dancing shoes just yet. However, Jesus kept on coming for me, and finally, I surrendered. I couldn't run anymore; my back was against the wall. It was time. He needed me to do his work, and I answered the call to do it.

I surrendered my life some years ago now and was born again through the baptism of his Holy Spirit. I could see God moving in my life, changing some of the things inside.

I experienced his truth because he came to me, and I know the difference between what I had before and what I was given. I wasn't speaking in tongues before; now, I have his holy Ghost, who has been such a great support for me. I speak boldly and am not afraid of what or who I say it to.

The most important thing is that he gave me identity and told me who I was appointed to be, and that gave me purpose and hope to keep on keeping on each day. Life was heavy at times I struggled off the weight of a deep sorrow keeping me down, but God's grace has been keeping me and telling me you got this.

Jesus came to change things for the better and for his purpose alone. I love having faith in God. I wouldn't be here if I didn't have faith. It is a vital part of my being. I know that the journey isn't always an easy journey because being tested and tried is part of it, so we are refined and better than before. So, I have faith because I truly believe in God because he showed up and let me know he is real in my life.

Now, let us look at your life and see if you witness the manifestation of God's presence, his saving grace, or even his love in your life. If we look back and recollect the past times, we may be able to see him all along.

Faith in God is important because if we pray to God and ask him to heal or deliver us from someone or something, and we doubt that he'll come through. Then, we don't rely on or even believe he is our healer or deliverance. For everyone whom Jesus delivered without even going to the person's place, he'd say, "Faith made them strong." Therefore, faith is required if you are seeking God.

"And Jesus answered them, "Have faith in God. Truly, I say to you, whoever says to this mountain, 'Be taken up and thrown into the sea, 'and does not doubt in his heart but believes that what he says will come to pass, it will be done for him. Therefore, I tell you, whatever you ask in prayer, believe that you have received it, and it will be yours." **(Mark 11:22-24).**

The scripture states that we aren't to have doubt in our hearts, and whatever we say will come to pass. So, if you don't believe in God but say you do with your mouth, it will manifest whether you speak truthfully because the thing will be done according to his word.

Our hearts and our mouths have to be on the same page. Otherwise, your heart will doubt, and you will speak about getting God to do something you don't believe he will do for you.

The disciples had to ask for an increase of Faith when they were lacking, or if you have doubt or fear, even concerns about trusting God. Bring those concerns to him so he can help you with them. "The apostles said to the Lord, "Increase our faith!" **(Luke 17:5).**

That is why we need God's wisdom in everything, and we can ask him to give us this. Just as King Solomon discerned his needs at the moment was for wisdom, we can seek this for ourselves.

"If any of you lacks wisdom, let him ask God, who gives generously to all without reproach, and it will be given him. But let him ask in faith, with no doubting, for the one who doubts is like a wave of the sea driven and tossed by the wind. For that person must not suppose that he will receive anything from the Lord; he is a double-minded man, unstable in all his ways." (**James 1:5-8**).

Just having faith and believing only, is part of what is required. We must take the necessary actions as stated in **James 2:14-26** – "What good is it, my brothers if someone says he has faith but does not have works? Can that faith save him?

If a brother or sister is poorly clothed and lacking in daily food, and one of you says to them," Go in peace, be warmed and filled, "Without giving them the things needed for the body, what good is that?" So also, faith by itself, if it does not have works, is dead. But someone will say, "You have faith and I have works. Show me your faith apart from your works, and I will show you my faith by my works."

So, we cannot just believe. We have to demonstrate those beliefs. If it is in the power of our hands to give and help someone, then we should do this. This isn't like magic. We believe, and then speak it and poof, it shows up. Like someone is hungry, and we just made food, but we send them away, saying be filled when we could have fixed them a plate of the food you had.

The thing is, you may think we don't have enough to share, but just like the story in the bible with the 5 loaves of bread and 2 fishes, God blessed that food and fed a multitude of people. The story even states that the people ate enough until they were full and still had leftovers. So, we need not to worry. God will supply all of our needs; we just need to trust him.

God loves when his children can rely on him and trust his character. That's what he says he will surely do because he isn't slack on his promises like we tend to do to each other. However, he is true to his word and will do what he will do on his time. However, he is shown strong in our lives when we activate our faith. He will move mountains, open doors, and bring a dead man back alive.

Do we believe that in today's time, when we see so much chaos, we tend to question God, asking, "How come? Why? "For we walk by faith, not by sight." **(2 Corinthians 5:7)** We cannot go with what we see because the apostle Peter was walking on water when he looked to the Lord, but as soon as he took his eyes off him, he began to sink.

We see too much to rely on just what we perceive. There are deeper things going on that will surely be made plain one day. Today, we just have to remain focused on the one who can surely make sure we are doing well as long as we keep fighting the good fight of faith.

Let's Connect: Spirituality is so important for me to survive in this world. Without it is like having no water, or no darkness to sleep, hungry from no food. It is necessary, and though my faith may need increasing at times, just ask, and you shall receive.

Let's talk about it:

Do you find it hard at times to keep your faith?

Have you ever prayed for something, believing God can do it, but still, it didn't happen? If so, how did that affect your faith?

Have you ever needed to ask God to increase your faith?

How important is faith for you in today's time?

Hope for the hopeless

We hear this all the time: "I hope things get better," "I hope it works out." We hope for things because we don't see them or know if they are going to happen, but having hope is important because we are expecting something.

I think having hope is promising at a time when things don't look up. Or life hasn't gotten better for you since the pandemic. Things have become so expensive that we are afraid to move because rent is higher than normal, or the cost of living itself has skyrocketed, and we cannot afford things like before.

"Now faith is the assurance of things hoped for, the conviction of things not seen" **(Hebrew 11:1)**

So, we need faith to give us that assurance of the things we hoped for and haven't seen happen to us as yet. Like if you are looking to get this job you applied for and you believe in faith this is the job you are hoping to get. You have to keep your hope alive that your faith in God can open this door for you, and it will work out.

A lot of people may feel like I've been hoping for things, and nothing is working out. What is the matter? Is God not willing to fulfill my desires? He says in **Jeremiah 29:11**, " For I know the plans I have for you, declares the LORD, plans for welfare and not for evil, to give you a future and a hope." I've heard this scripture so much in my life.

I hope that this was as inspiring to you as it was to me. When I can see God doesn't have plans for us to fail, some opportunities we seek may not be for us. It could be God's way of letting you know he has better in store for you. This is where trust plays a big factor in believing that God knows best and does the best as well. He wants to give us a future and a hope.

According to **Romans 8:25** - "But if we hope for what we do not see, we wait for it with patience."

"Be strong, and let your heart take courage, all you who wait for the Lord!." **(Psalm 31:24)**

Sometimes, the hope we have to see change may take a long time to come because we are waiting on God, and he does it in his timing, which is right. We may not understand why because we asked for this yesterday, and still, it isn't here yet, but we can believe that God is true to his word. So, we have to let our heart take courage because it will feel at times to just give up or give in. Be strong, and be patient as well because we'll need it when all we have is hope.

Psalms 147:11 states, "But the Lord takes pleasure in those who fear him, in those who hope in his steadfast love."

We'll be those people who hope in God's steadfast love. He truly cares about what we are going through so do not worry yourself. Instead, know that God wants to help you as nothing is impossible for him to do. Everything will come together in due time.

For those who have experienced so much hopelessness, I know it is difficult to look up from how low you have been. However, if you hold on to hope for a better tomorrow to a God who can deliver on your behalf, we have something to look forward to.

We can only go as low as the floor, but then we have to climb back up again, and you can do it. You aren't alone through the difficulty, and you need that inner strength to help you regain that drive to hope again and live.

I've been there, feeling hopeless because my situation wasn't changing as quickly as I wanted it to. I just surrendered because I don't understand everything, and not everything will be explained in my time. We just have to keep trusting in him, having faith that he will surely bring us out.

With God, he has a greater purpose we may not always agree to, but in **Romans 8:28,** "Not only that, but we rejoice in our sufferings, knowing that suffering produces endurance, and endurance produces character, and character produces hope." **(Romans 5:3-5)**

I'd like to leave you with these last words by the late Martin Luther King Jr.: "We must accept finite disappointment, but never lose infinite hope."

Let's connect: I will never lose hope; it is what keeps me going each day. I hope for a better tomorrow, as each day has different things to offer. The sky may be dark at times, but the sun will surely shine once again.

Let's talk about it:

"What are your hopes?

Do you feel that your faith would allow you to obtain what you are hoping for?

"Have you ever been disappointed because you didn't get what you hoped for?"

Imagine if you were hoping for a green car but ended up with a yellow one. How would you feel?

Living for God

"Therefore, if anyone is in Christ, he is a new creation. The old has passed away; behold, the new has come." (*2 Corinthians 5:17*)

For If we live, we live to the Lord, and if we die, we die to the Lord. So then, whether we live or whether we die, we are the Lord's. **(Romans 14:8)**

Blessed assurance to know that we are yours, and you are ours. To know that our entire existence falls in the hands of God and that is reassuring. No matter what we face, there is a brighter day to come because, with God, trouble won't always last. With God, he will fight all of our battles, and we won't have to face life alone.

The most comforting thing is that God wants to have fellowship with us. He created us with the intention in mind that we'd live in one with him. He provided us leadership to be in charge of his earthly affairs; we'd have a commune with him in the spirit. Living a bountiful life together, you can see the picture from the beginning of creation. His plan didn't quite work out as he expected it to, as we know. Then we became sinful in nature, and this isn't God's character as he is a holy God. So, Jesus is God's reconciliation to return to having this fellowship with God again.

"For Christ also suffered once for sins, the righteous for the unrighteous, that he might bring us to God, being put to death in the flesh but made alive in the spirit, in which he went and proclaimed to the spirits in prison because they formerly did not obey, when God's patience waited in the days of Noah, while the ark was being prepared, in which a few, that is, eight persons, were brought safely through water. Baptism, which corresponds to this, now saves you, not as a removal of dirt from the body but as an appeal to God for a good conscience through the resurrection of Jesus Christ, who has gone into heaven and is at the right hand of God, with angels, authorities, and powers having been subjected to him." **(1 Peter 3:18-22)**

We've battled through trying times such as COVID-19, where we faced so many uncertainties and lost loved ones along the way, but we must keep trusting in God. It isn't over, but it is far from where we began. "When I am afraid, I put my trust in you. In God, whose word I praise, in God I trust; I shall not be afraid. What can flesh do to me?" **(Psalm 56:3-4)**

Let's keep on believing and loving each other now that we have the chance to.

Giving our lives means giving ourselves, our body, mind and spirit, our finances, and every aspect of ourselves to God. To use for his purpose and glory. As he says in **1 Thessalonians 5:23**, "Now may the God of peace himself sanctify you completely, and may your whole spirit and soul and body be kept blameless at the coming of our Lord Jesus Christ."

You have to commit because it's once again your choice (free will is yours). After an experience like COVID-19, which attacked the world at large, we had to change a number of external things, like sanitizing our hands, social distancing, and so forth. However, with God, he wants to change the internal things of our beings.

We have three things that we can use to commit to God: our Body, Mind, and Spirit.

Now, the thing is, if we were to consider giving this to just anyone, we'd have to ponder and wonder if they are the right person to do this with. Knowing that we are still holding on to a hand, we cannot see with our physical eyes, but things are moving for our best. He can heal and keep your body, mind, and spirit.

You are in the best hands, my friends, if you'd know that life is in his hands as we remember that song, "He's got the whole world in his hands." He's got you and me in his hands, the whole wide world in his hands."

Good loves communion with his creation, everything working in oneness, he set everything in motion for it to follow his timely command. However, the one thing he gives to us is freedom of choice whether we'd choose him.

He wants all of us to be a part of his will, but it is up to us to decide whether we'd take up our own crosses and follow him. If you were to surrender all of your beings, all of your life, to him, you'd be giving this to the best person because you are his greatest creation of them all.

Your life won't be empty but filled with God's goodness for those who want to walk and embrace this life with him. We are again alive to do so now because after we are gone, there is no opportunity, so let him be proud of you now and come fully into acceptance to have this great relationship with your father.

We can live as we have the breath; we breathe, but let it count and matter so we are the best versions of God, ourselves, and others as well.

Praise the Lord for the great things he has done.

Let us continue to live the breath of life, a fantastic gift from God himself, all in Jesus Christ.

Inhale..........

To a loving God who always cared for us and did something about it. He gave us his only son. We are created for him, by him, for his purpose alone. We are all needed in his kingdom. "For many are called, but few are chosen." **(Matthew 22:14)**

Will you answer to the call of your life?

Exhale............

Glory be to God.

Let's connect: To live in communion with God was his initial plan. His heart broke for us, and he still fixed it again. Doing what was so painful but overall purposeful. He was intentional and did something about it. What will you do this very moment?

Let's talk about it:

What does a life with God look like to you?

Are there things you still need clarity on? If so, what are those things?

Do you see the value of having God in your life?

Is there anything you still would like to know before you live fully for God?

The End

In closing, before I came up with the idea of writing this book, it all started with a thought: How dare a disease as deadly as COVID-19 come and take the very thing God gave to us, the breath of life? Then I began to write. I hope that reading this book took you on a journey to see the importance of God our Father and the power he can truly provide to your life.

He is truly the air that we breath, and breathe that gives us the life we live today. Everything about us demonstrates his love and existence. Importantly, he created us in his image. Because without him, there would be no us.

We all share a part of the same story when we can say we went through the pandemic (COVID-19). We witnessed how it turned the entire world upside down, but we still overcame it and have life today. I am truly blessed and happy that we are still here to run the race of life together. We can get through a lot, as we have seen the collectiveness we had as we pulled through this devastation, but we all played our part, and now we see the results of this.

The biggest question to ask ourselves is, "How do I live this life now?" after all, God has brought us through. We don't just want to live but to live intentionally and with purpose. God needs each and every one of us to tap into the greatness he instilled inside of us. I once heard someone say "that the graveyard is one of the wealthiest places." Because so many people leave Earth with all God invested in them. That song they didn't write could have brought life changes and deliverance, a story they could have written but never got to or were fearful to even start.

That business idea would have been life-changing. But for whatever reason, it wasn't done. We don't want to be like that; we have to find our calling and use the gifts God gave us to fulfill his will. So, at the end of our task, we can say, like Jesus did, " It is finished." I did what I was sent to do.

Also, God wants to be apart of your life through the ups and downs. He wants to be involved and for everyone to reach repentance and be saved through his son, Jesus Christ.

You are important to him and the mighty works he wants to fulfill on earth. Avail yourself to him as he is ready to have a relationship with you only if you are ready.

We have to search our lives and see the goodness of God. He can be found if we truly look to see him.

Let's pray

God, we thank you for being our creator and for thinking about us before we can think of ourselves. You did for us what no other can do for us, and we are grateful for you being in our lives.

We are grateful to experience your love and receive your free love for all in need and who wants you. Thank you for creating us and doing it so well. We are so intrigued by your handiwork and that we are created in your image and likeness. Thank you for bringing us through many trials and tribulations, especially the pandemic. We are here today because you kept us alive for your perfect will. You saved us from losing the perfect gift you provided to us, which we cannot take for granted, which is the gift of life. Give us the wisdom to live our lives for you, taking care of our body, mind and spirit. Giving us the knowledge to get to know you better, and understanding to know how we are to apply what we've learned to our lives.

We have a story of our triumphs and victory in your name, Lord, and for this, we are truly at peace. You have shown that you are our protector, and we are safe in you. Teach us how to continue to love you and love others as you have shown us love.

Your word is a lamp to our feet guiding us on how we are to maneuver through the most conflicting times of our lives. We don't need to question your authority when we are faced with life's blows of sickness, trials and tribulations because we trust and believe in your supernatural power.

We receive your spirit of joy, peace and love into our hearts. We open ourselves to receive the abundant life you will give us as long as you are the center of our lives.

All of my days my attitude will be sincere gratitude for what you have done for me and my family, and those who overcame. The blessing you bestow upon me will flow onto others so they, too, can taste and see that you are a good God.

Your love is what ushers me into your presence and allows me to know that this is a way of life. We should choose to love you and others as I love myself. You had increased my faith when I didn't know I needed to and displayed your wonders in my life when I believed and put in the work to allow you to move in our lives.

We wouldn't be here today if it wasn't for your Grace and mercy, and we chose to surrender our walk of life to your hands for your will and purpose. In your hands, I will be well taken care of, and I am happy to serve you, Lord, my savior. Thank you for your victory. In Jesus' name, we pray, Amen.

Now, go on and walk in your victory. We got this!!!

www.ingramcontent.com/pod-product-compliance
Lightning Source LLC
Chambersburg PA
CBHW020411130626
46549CB00006B/2519